Sunday School Lessons for Teens

(13-19 yrs)

A Bible-Based Guide for Connecting Faith and Life in a Modern World

Ruth Prints

Table of contents

INTRODUCTION

Sunday School is a sacred space where teenagers embark on a journey of spiritual growth, exploration, and discovery. Rooted in biblical teachings and designed specifically for the unique needs of adolescents, Sunday School serves as a cornerstone in nurturing their faith, character, and relationship with God. In this comprehensive guide, we delve into the significance of Sunday School for teens, strategies for engaging them in meaningful discussions, and the importance of fostering a safe and inclusive environment where they can thrive.

Understanding the Purpose of Sunday School for Teens

Sunday School holds a pivotal role in the spiritual formation of teenagers, providing them with a solid foundation in biblical knowledge and principles that guide their beliefs and actions. As adolescents navigate the complexities of adolescence and grapple with questions of identity, purpose, and belonging, Sunday School offers a nurturing environment where they can explore these themes through the lens of Scripture. At its core, the purpose of Sunday School for teens is to foster spiritual growth and maturity. Through interactive lessons, discussions, and activities, teenagers are encouraged to deepen their understanding of God's Word and apply its timeless truths to their lives. By studying the stories of faith-filled heroes and heroines in the Bible, such as David,

Esther, and Paul, teens are inspired to emulate their courage, resilience, and unwavering trust in God.

Moreover, Sunday School equips teenagers with the knowledge, skills, and spiritual gifts necessary for serving others and fulfilling their God-given calling. Through service projects, mission trips, and leadership opportunities, they discover the joy and fulfillment that comes from using their gifts to make a difference in the world.

How to Engage Teenagers in Meaningful Discussions

Engaging teenagers in meaningful discussions requires intentionality, creativity, and sensitivity to their unique needs and interests. By employing a variety of interactive teaching methods and incorporating relevant topics and issues, Sunday School leaders can capture the attention and participation of teens, fostering a deeper understanding and application of biblical truths.

Interactive Teaching Methods: One effective strategy for engaging teenagers in meaningful discussions is to utilize interactive teaching methods that encourage active participation and critical thinking. Rather than relying solely on lectures or monologues, Sunday School leaders can incorporate group discussions, small group activities, role-playing, multimedia presentations, and hands-on projects to create dynamic and engaging learning experiences. By allowing teens to express their thoughts, questions, and insights, they feel valued and empowered to take ownership of their learning journey.

Relevant and Real-Life Applications: Another key aspect of engaging teenagers in meaningful discussions is to make connections between biblical principles and real-life situations that resonate with their lived experiences. Sunday School leaders can explore contemporary issues such as peer pressure, relationships, social media, mental health, and cultural diversity through the lens of Scripture, helping teens to see the relevance and applicability of God's Word to their everyday lives. By providing practical guidance and insights, teens are equipped to navigate the challenges and complexities of adolescence with wisdom and discernment.

Openness and Authenticity: Finally, fostering an atmosphere of openness, authenticity, and trust is essential for engaging teenagers in meaningful discussions. Sunday School leaders should create a safe and welcoming environment where teens feel comfortable expressing their doubts, struggles, and questions without fear of judgment or condemnation. By modeling vulnerability and transparency, adult leaders can cultivate a culture of authenticity and mutual respect, where teens are free to wrestle with difficult issues and explore their faith journey at their own pace.

Creating a Safe and Inclusive Environment

Creating a safe and inclusive environment is paramount in Sunday School settings, where teenagers can encounter God's love, grace, and truth in a nurturing and supportive community. By prioritizing the physical, emotional, and spiritual well-being of teens, Sunday School leaders lay the foundation for a transformative and life-giving experience where all are welcomed and valued.

Emotional Support and Care: It is essential to provide emotional support and care for teenagers who may be facing various challenges and struggles in their lives. Sunday School leaders should cultivate an atmosphere of empathy, compassion, and understanding, where teens feel heard, valued, and supported in their joys and sorrows. By offering prayer, encouragement, and practical assistance, adult leaders demonstrate God's love and concern for the holistic well-being of each teenager.

Spiritual Nourishment and Growth: Creating a safe and inclusive environment involves nurturing the spiritual growth and development of teenagers in a manner that affirms their unique identities and experiences. Sunday School leaders should celebrate diversity and inclusivity, embracing teens from all backgrounds, cultures, and walks of life with warmth and acceptance. By incorporating diverse perspectives, voices, and stories into the curriculum and discussions, teens gain a broader understanding of God's love and purpose for humanity, transcending cultural barriers and divisions.

In conclusion, Sunday School for teens is a sacred and transformative journey where young people encounter God's truth, grace, and love in a supportive and nurturing community. By understanding the purpose of Sunday School, engaging teenagers in meaningful discussions, and creating a safe and inclusive environment, we empower them to grow in faith, character, and service, equipping them to impact their world for Christ.

Lesson 1

Creation and the Importance of Stewardship

Scripture: Genesis 1:1-31, Genesis 2:15.

Memory Verse: Genesis 1:31a - "God saw all that he had made, and it was very good."

Exposition

In the beginning, God created the heavens and the earth. This foundational truth, as revealed in the book of Genesis, lays the groundwork for understanding the significance of creation and the role of humanity as stewards of God's magnificent handiwork. Before delving into the intricacies of stewardship, it is essential to define two key concepts: creation and stewardship.

Creation refers to the act by which God brought the universe and all living things into existence out of nothing. In Genesis 1, we read the majestic account of God's creative work, as he spoke the world into being over the course of six days. From the splendor of the heavens to the beauty of the earth, every aspect of creation reflects the wisdom, power, and goodness of God.

Stewardship, on the other hand, encompasses the responsible management and care of God's creation entrusted to humanity. As stewards, we are called to recognize that the earth and everything in it ultimately belong to God, and we are entrusted with the privilege and responsibility of caring for it on his behalf. Stewardship is not merely about preserving natural resources or environmental conservation; it is a holistic way of life that acknowledges our interconnectedness with all of God's creation and our responsibility to honor and protect it.

Discuss Questions

1. What does it mean to be a steward of God's creation?
2. How does our understanding of creation shape our worldview and our relationship with the environment?
3. In what ways can we demonstrate stewardship in our daily lives, both individually and collectively?
4. What are some biblical examples of individuals or communities practicing stewardship in the Old and New Testaments?

Lesson 2

Noah's Ark and Trusting God's Promises

Scripture: Genesis 6:9-22, Genesis 7:1-24, Genesis 8:1-22, Genesis 9:1-17.

Memory Verse: Genesis 9:16 - "Whenever the rainbow appears in the clouds, I will see it and remember the everlasting covenant between God and all living creatures of every kind on the earth."

Exposition

The story of Noah's Ark is one of the most iconic narratives in the Bible, illustrating the themes of obedience, faith, and God's faithfulness in the face of adversity. At its core, the account of Noah and the flood highlights the importance of trusting in God's promises and following his commands, even when they seem difficult or improbable.

Before exploring the details of Noah's Ark, it is crucial to understand the context in which this event takes place. In Genesis 6, we learn that the wickedness of humanity had reached such depths that God, in his righteous judgment, decided to bring a flood upon the earth to cleanse it of sin and corruption. However, amidst the prevailing darkness, Noah found favor in the eyes of the Lord, being described as a righteous man who walked faithfully with God.

Discuss Questions

1. What qualities did Noah possess that made him stand out in his generation?
2. How did Noah demonstrate his faith and obedience to God in building the ark?
3. What challenges and obstacles did Noah face as he embarked on this monumental task?
4. What can we learn from Noah's example about trusting in God's promises and obeying his commands, even when they seem difficult or unpopular?
5. How does the covenant God made with Noah after the flood reassure us of his faithfulness and enduring love for his creation?

Lesson 3

Abraham's Faith Journey

Scripture: Genesis 12:1-9, Genesis 15:1-6, Genesis 17:1-8, Genesis 22:1-19

Memory Verse: Genesis 15:6 - "Abram believed the Lord, and he credited it to him as righteousness."

Exposition

The story of Abraham, often referred to as the father of faith, is a compelling narrative that spans several chapters in the book of Genesis. Abraham's faith journey serves as a profound example of trusting in God's promises and following his lead, even when the path ahead is uncertain and filled with obstacles.

Abraham's journey of faith begins with a call from God to leave his homeland and embark on a journey to a land that God would show him. In Genesis 12, we read of God's covenant with Abraham, promising to bless him, make his name great, and bless all the families of the earth through him. Despite the challenges and uncertainties that lay ahead, Abraham obediently followed God's command, demonstrating unwavering faith and trust in God's promises.

Discuss Questions

1. What initial challenges did Abraham face when God called him to leave his homeland and journey to a land that God would show him?
2. How did Abraham respond to God's promises, particularly regarding his descendants and the land of Canaan?
3. What obstacles and trials did Abraham encounter along his faith journey, and how did he respond to them?
4. What role did faith play in Abraham's relationship with God, and how did his faith evolve and deepen over time?
5. How does Abraham's faith journey inspire us to trust in God's promises and step out in faith, even when the path ahead is uncertain?

Lesson 4

Moses and the Power of Perseverance

Scripture: Exodus 2:1-10, Exodus 3:1-15, Exodus 14:5-31, Deuteronomy 34:1-12.

Memory Verse: Exodus 14:14 - "The Lord will fight for you; you need only to be still."

Exposition

The story of Moses is one of courage, perseverance, and divine intervention. From his miraculous rescue as an infant to his leadership of the Israelites out of slavery in Egypt, Moses' life exemplifies the power of perseverance in the face of adversity and the faithfulness of God in fulfilling his promises.

Moses' journey begins in the midst of oppression and persecution, as the Israelites suffer under the cruel bondage of Pharaoh in Egypt. Despite being raised in the palace as the son of Pharaoh's daughter, Moses identifies with his oppressed brethren and ultimately chooses to stand with them, even at great personal risk. In Exodus 3, we read of God's call to Moses from the burning bush, commissioning him to lead the Israelites out of Egypt and into the Promised Land. Despite his initial reluctance and self-doubt, Moses ultimately embraces his calling and becomes a powerful instrument of God's deliverance for his people.

Discuss Questions

1. What were some of the challenges and obstacles that Moses faced in his life, both before and after his call from God?

2. How did Moses demonstrate perseverance and faithfulness in his leadership of the Israelites, particularly during their journey through the wilderness?

3. What lessons can we learn from Moses' example about trusting in God's guidance and provision, even when the path ahead seems daunting and uncertain?

4. How did God demonstrate his faithfulness and power through the various miracles and signs performed during Moses' ministry, such as the plagues of Egypt and the parting of the Red Sea?

5. How does Moses' story inspire us to persevere in our own faith journey, trusting in God's promises and relying on his strength to overcome obstacles and challenges?

Lesson 5

David and Goliath: Facing Giants in Life

Scripture
- 1 Samuel 17:1-58

Memory Verse
- 1 Samuel 17:45 - "You come against me with sword and spear and javelin, but I come against you in the name of the Lord Almighty, the God of the armies of Israel, whom you have defied."

Exposition

The story of David and Goliath is a timeless tale of courage, faith, and overcoming insurmountable odds through the power of God. Set against the backdrop of the Israelites' ongoing conflict with the Philistines, this narrative illustrates the importance of trusting in God's strength and standing firm in the face of adversity.

The giant Goliath, a formidable champion of the Philistine army, taunts and intimidates the Israelites, challenging them to send forth a champion to face him in single combat. Despite the fear and hesitation of King Saul and his army, a young shepherd boy named David steps forward to accept the challenge, armed only with his sling and a few stones. With unwavering faith in God's power and deliverance, David confronts Goliath on the battlefield and emerges victorious, striking down the mighty giant with a single stone.

Discuss Questions

1. What factors contributed to David's courage and confidence in facing Goliath, despite his young age and lack of military experience?
2. How did David's trust in God's strength and provision enable him to overcome his fear and confront Goliath head-on?
3. What lessons can we learn from David's example about the importance of relying on God's power and promises in times of adversity?
4. In what ways do we encounter "giants" or challenges in our own lives, and how can David's story inspire us to face them with courage and faith?

Lesson 6

Esther: Courage in Times of Crisis

Scripture: Esther 2:1-18, Esther 4:1-17, Esther 5:1-8, Esther 7:1-10

Memory Verse
- Esther 4:14b - "And who knows but that you have come to your royal position for such a time as this?"

Exposition

The story of Esther is a captivating narrative of courage, faith, and divine providence amidst a time of crisis and uncertainty. Set against the backdrop of ancient Persia, Esther, a young Jewish woman, finds herself thrust into a position of influence and authority as queen, tasked with saving her people from destruction at the hands of the wicked Haman.

Esther's journey begins with her unlikely rise to prominence, as she is chosen from among many young women to become queen of Persia. However, her newfound position of power comes with great responsibility, as she discovers a plot by Haman to annihilate the Jewish people throughout the empire. Despite the risks and dangers involved, Esther demonstrates remarkable courage and faith as she boldly approaches the King to plead for the salvation of her people.

Discuss Questions

1. What qualities and characteristics did Esther possess that made her an effective leader and advocate for her people?
2. How did Esther's faith in God's providence and guidance empower her to take decisive action in the face of danger and uncertainty?
3. What risks and sacrifices did Esther face in confronting King Xerxes and exposing Haman's plot against the Jewish people?
4. In what ways did God's hand of providence and deliverance manifest throughout Esther's story, from her rise to queen to the defeat of her enemies?
5. How does Esther's story inspire us to trust in God's sovereignty and guidance, even when faced with seemingly insurmountable obstacles and challenges?

Lesson 7

Jonah and the Call to Obedience

Scripture: Jonah 1:1-17, Jonah 2:1-10, Jonah 3:1-10, Jonah 4:1-11

Memory Verse
- Jonah 2:9 - "But I, with shouts of grateful praise, will sacrifice to you. What I have vowed I will make good. I will say, 'Salvation comes from the Lord.'"

Exposition

The story of Jonah is a captivating account of God's relentless pursuit of his wayward prophet and the call to obedience, even in the face of fear, disobedience, and rebellion. Through Jonah's experiences, we learn valuable lessons about the consequences of disobedience, the importance of repentance, and the boundless mercy and compassion of God.

Jonah, a prophet of Israel, receives a divine commission from God to go to the great city of Nineveh and proclaim a message of judgment against its wickedness. However, instead of obeying God's command, Jonah flees in the opposite direction, boarding a ship bound for Tarshish. Yet, God's sovereignty and providence are evident throughout Jonah's journey, as he encounters a violent storm at sea, is swallowed by a great fish, and ultimately brought to repentance and obedience.

Discuss Questions

1. What were some of the reasons why Jonah initially resisted God's call to go to Nineveh and preach repentance to its people?
2. How did Jonah's disobedience and rebellion affect those around him, including the sailors on the ship and the people of Nineveh?
3. What lessons can we learn from Jonah's experiences about the consequences of disobedience and the importance of repentance and obedience to God's will?
4. How did God demonstrate his mercy and compassion towards Jonah, even in the midst of his rebellion and disobedience?

Lesson 8

Daniel's Integrity in a World of Compromise

Scripture: Daniel 1:1-21, Daniel 2:1-23, Daniel 6:1-28

Memory Verse
- Daniel 6:10b - "Three times a day he got down on his knees and prayed, giving thanks to his God, just as he had done before."

Exposition

The story of Daniel and his companions is a powerful testament to the importance of maintaining integrity and faithfulness to God in the midst of a culture that seeks to compromise and conform to worldly standards. Through their unwavering commitment to obedience and devotion to God, Daniel and his friends exemplify the transformative power of living with integrity and conviction in a world of compromise.

As young Israelites taken into exile in Babylon, Daniel and his companions find themselves confronted with numerous challenges to their faith and identity. Yet, rather than succumbing to the pressures and temptations of their surroundings, they remain steadfast in their commitment to

God and his commandments, refusing to compromise their principles or defile themselves with the king's food and wine.

Discuss Questions

1. What were some of the pressures and temptations that Daniel and his friends faced in Babylon, and how did they respond with integrity and faithfulness to God?

2. How did Daniel's commitment to prayer and dependence on God's wisdom and guidance enable him to interpret the king's dreams and receive divine revelation?

3. What risks and consequences did Daniel and his friends face for their refusal to compromise their faith and principles, particularly in the face of King Nebuchadnezzar and King Darius?

4. In what ways did God demonstrate his faithfulness and protection towards Daniel and his friends, even in the midst of persecution and opposition?

5. How does Daniel's example of integrity and faithfulness challenge us to stand firm in our own convictions and principles, even when faced with pressure to compromise or conform to the standards of the world?

Lesson 9

The Birth of Jesus: Emmanuel, God With Us

Scripture: Matthew 1:18-25, Luke 2:1-20, John 1:1-14

Memory Verse
- Matthew 1:23 - "Behold, the virgin shall conceive and bear a son, and they shall call his name Immanuel (which means, God with us)."

Exposition

The birth of Jesus Christ is a pivotal moment in human history, marking the fulfillment of God's promise to send a Savior to redeem and reconcile humanity to himself. The incarnation of Jesus as Immanuel, meaning "God with us," embodies the profound truth of God's presence and love manifested in human form. Through the miraculous events surrounding Jesus' birth, we witness the convergence of divine intervention and human vulnerability, as God enters into the brokenness and darkness of our world to bring hope, salvation, and eternal life.

In Matthew's gospel, we read of the angel's announcement to Joseph, informing him of Mary's miraculous conception by the Holy Spirit and the significance of the child she carries. In Luke's gospel, we encounter the humble circumstances of Jesus' birth in Bethlehem, where he is laid in a manger amidst shepherds and angels proclaiming the good news of his arrival. And in John's gospel, we are reminded of the eternal nature of Jesus as the Word made flesh, dwelling among us in fullness of grace and truth.

Discuss Questions

1. What do the accounts of Jesus' birth in the gospels of Matthew, Luke, and John reveal about the nature and significance of his incarnation as Immanuel, God with us?
2. How does Jesus' birth fulfill the Old Testament prophecies and promises concerning the coming Messiah and Savior of the world?
3. In what ways does the birth of Jesus demonstrate God's love and compassion towards humanity, as expressed through his willingness to enter into our world and share in our human experience?
4. What lessons can we learn from the circumstances surrounding Jesus' birth, such as the humility of his earthly parents, the response of the shepherds, and the worship of the Magi?

Lesson 10

Jesus' Ministry: Love in Action

Scripture: Matthew 4:12-25, Mark 1:14-39, Luke 4:14-44, John 13:1-17

Memory Verse
- John 13:34-35 - "A new commandment I give to you, that you love one another: just as I have loved you, you also are to love one another. By this all people will know that you are my disciples, if you have love for one another."

Exposition

The ministry of Jesus Christ is characterized by love in action, as he demonstrates compassion, mercy, and healing towards those in need. From the shores of Galilee to the streets of Jerusalem, Jesus' ministry embodies the transformative power of love to heal, restore, and reconcile broken lives and communities. Through his words and deeds, Jesus invites us to follow his example of selfless love and service, both to God and to our neighbors.

In the synoptic gospels of Matthew, Mark, and Luke, we read of Jesus' public ministry, which begins with his baptism by

John the Baptist and culminates in his death and resurrection. Throughout his ministry, Jesus proclaims the kingdom of God, heals the sick, casts out demons, and teaches with authority and wisdom. In the gospel of John, we are given a glimpse into the heart of Jesus' ministry as he washes his disciples' feet and commands them to love one another as he has loved them.

Discuss Questions

1. What are some of the key aspects of Jesus' ministry as recorded in the gospels, and how do they demonstrate his love and compassion towards humanity?
2. How did Jesus' ministry challenge the religious and social norms of his time, particularly in his interactions with outcasts, sinners, and marginalized groups?
3. What lessons can we learn from Jesus' example of love in action, such as his healing miracles, teachings on forgiveness, and acts of service towards others?
4. In what ways does Jesus' commandment to love one another as he has loved us serve as the foundation for our discipleship and witness to the world?
5. How can we emulate Jesus' example of love in action in our own lives and communities, demonstrating God's love and compassion to those around us in practical and tangible ways?

Lesson 11

The Parable of the Good Samaritan: Compassion and Neighborly Love

Scripture
- Luke 10:25-37

Memory Verse
- Luke 10:37 - "Go and do likewise."

Exposition

The parable of the Good Samaritan is a timeless story of compassion, mercy, and neighborly love that challenges us to reexamine our attitudes towards those in need and our responsibilities as followers of Christ. Set against the backdrop of a conversation between Jesus and a legal expert seeking to justify himself, this parable reveals the radical nature of love and compassion that transcends social, cultural, and religious barriers.

In the parable, a man traveling from Jerusalem to Jericho is attacked by robbers and left half dead by the side of the road. Despite the religious and social conventions of the time, it is a despised Samaritan who demonstrates true compassion and mercy towards the wounded man, bandaging his wounds, caring for him, and providing for his needs. Through this simple yet profound act of kindness, Jesus illustrates the transformative power of love to bridge divides and restore dignity to those in need.

Discuss Questions

1. What are some of the key elements of the parable of the Good Samaritan, and how do they challenge our assumptions about compassion, mercy, and neighborly love?
2. What contrasts are highlighted in the parable between the actions of the Samaritan and those of the priest and the Levite, and what do these contrasts teach us about true compassion and righteousness?
3. In what ways does the parable challenge us to rethink our attitudes towards those who are different from us or marginalized in society, and to extend compassion and mercy to all, regardless of social, cultural, or religious distinctions?
4. How does Jesus' command to "go and do likewise" compel us to actively engage in acts of compassion and mercy towards those in need, both within and outside of our communities?
5. How can we apply the principles of the parable of the Good Samaritan in our own lives and contexts, demonstrating God's love and compassion to those around us in practical and tangible ways?

Lesson 12

The Sermon on the Mount: Living Out the Beatitudes

Scripture
- Matthew 5:1-12

Memory Verse
- Matthew 5:3 - "Blessed are the poor in spirit, for theirs is the kingdom of heaven."

Exposition

The Sermon on the Mount, delivered by Jesus Christ on a mountainside in Galilee, is one of the most iconic and influential teachings in all of Scripture. In this profound sermon, Jesus presents a vision for kingdom living that challenges conventional wisdom and calls his followers to embody attitudes and values that reflect the character of God. Central to the Sermon on the Mount are the Beatitudes, a series of blessings pronounced upon those who possess specific spiritual qualities and virtues.

As Jesus begins his sermon, he addresses the crowds gathered before him, proclaiming blessings upon the poor in spirit, the mourners, the meek, those who hunger and thirst for righteousness, the merciful, the pure in heart, the peacemakers, and those who are persecuted for righteousness' sake. Through these declarations of blessing, Jesus reveals the upside-down nature of God's kingdom, where the values of humility, mercy, righteousness, and peace are exalted above worldly power, wealth, and status.

Discuss Questions

1. What are the Beatitudes, and what do they reveal about the character and values of God's kingdom?
2. How do the Beatitudes challenge our conventional notions of happiness, success, and fulfillment, and invite us to embrace a different way of living and being in the world?
3. In what ways do the Beatitudes highlight the interconnectedness of spiritual virtues and qualities, such as humility, compassion, and purity of heart?
4. What does it mean to "live out" the Beatitudes in our daily lives, and how can we embody these attitudes and values in our relationships, actions, and choices?

Lesson 13

Jesus Calms the Storm: Finding Peace in Chaos

Scripture: Matthew 8:23-27, Mark 4:35-41, Luke 8:22-25

Memory Verse
- Mark 4:39 - "He got up, rebuked the wind and said to the waves, 'Quiet! Be still!' Then the wind died down and it was completely calm."

Exposition

The story of Jesus calming the storm is a powerful demonstration of his authority over nature and his ability to bring peace and calm in the midst of chaos and turmoil. Set against the backdrop of a violent storm on the Sea of Galilee, this miraculous event reveals Jesus' divine power and invites us to trust in him as the one who can calm the storms of our lives and bring us peace in the midst of adversity.

As Jesus and his disciples set out across the sea, a fierce storm suddenly arises, threatening to capsize their boat and drown them. In their fear and desperation, the disciples awaken Jesus, who rebukes the wind and the waves with a single command, "Quiet! Be still!" Immediately, the storm ceases, and the sea becomes calm, leaving the disciples in awe of Jesus' power and authority over creation.

Discuss Questions

1. What factors contributed to the fear and panic of the disciples as they encountered the storm on the Sea of Galilee?
2. How did Jesus demonstrate his authority over nature and his ability to bring peace in the midst of chaos through his actions in calming the storm?
3. In what ways does the story of Jesus calming the storm serve as a metaphor for the challenges and trials we face in our own lives, and the assurance of God's presence and power to bring us peace and deliverance?
4. How can we cultivate a deeper sense of trust and faith in Jesus as the one who can calm the storms of our lives and bring us peace in the midst of adversity?
5. What are some practical steps we can take to find peace and serenity in God's presence, even when faced with turbulent circumstances and uncertainty?

Lesson 14

The Woman at the Well: Finding Fulfillment in Christ

Scripture
- John 4:1-42

Memory Verse
- John 4:14 - "But whoever drinks the water I give them will never thirst. Indeed, the water I give them will become in them a spring of water welling up to eternal life."

Exposition

The encounter between Jesus and the woman at the well is a poignant and transformative interaction that illustrates the depth of God's love and the offer of living water that satisfies the deepest longings of the human heart. Set against the backdrop of Jacob's well in Samaria, this encounter reveals Jesus' radical inclusion and acceptance of all people, regardless of their social status, ethnicity, or past mistakes.

As Jesus sits by the well, weary from his journey, he encounters a Samaritan woman who has come to draw water. In their conversation, Jesus offers her living water, symbolic of the spiritual refreshment and eternal life that he alone can provide. As their dialogue unfolds, Jesus reveals the woman's deepest secrets and desires, leading her to recognize him as the long-awaited Messiah and inviting her to drink from the wellspring of his grace and salvation.

Discuss Questions

1. What were some of the cultural and religious barriers that existed between Jesus and the woman at the well, and how did Jesus break down these barriers through his actions and words?

2. How did Jesus address the woman's spiritual thirst and offer her living water that satisfies the deepest longings of her heart?

3. In what ways does the encounter between Jesus and the woman at the well challenge our preconceptions about who is worthy of God's love and grace, and invite us to embrace a posture of radical inclusion and acceptance towards others?

4. What lessons can we learn from the woman's response to Jesus' offer of living water, as she recognizes him as the Messiah and shares her newfound faith with others?

5. How can we experience the fulfillment and satisfaction that comes from knowing Christ as our Savior and Redeemer, and how can we share this life-giving message with those around us who are spiritually thirsty and longing for meaning and purpose in their lives?

Lesson 15

The Prodigal Son: Understanding God's Unconditional Love

Scripture
- Luke 15:11-32

Memory Verse
- Luke 15:20b - "But while he was still a long way off, his father saw him and was filled with compassion for him; he ran to his son, threw his arms around him and kissed him."

Exposition

The parable of the Prodigal Son is a timeless story of redemption, forgiveness, and the boundless love of our Heavenly Father. Set against the backdrop of a wayward son who squanders his inheritance on reckless living, this parable reveals the depth of God's unconditional love and his longing for reconciliation with his lost children. Through the extravagant grace and mercy shown by the father towards his wayward son, we catch a glimpse of the Father heart of God and the invitation to come home to his loving embrace.

As Jesus tells the parable, he paints a vivid picture of a father who eagerly awaits the return of his wayward son, scanning the horizon each day in anticipation of his homecoming. When the son finally comes to his senses and returns home, broken and repentant, the father's response is one of extravagant love and compassion. He welcomes his son with open arms, throws a lavish celebration in his honor, and restores him to his rightful place in the family.

Discuss Questions

1. What aspects of the parable of the Prodigal Son resonate with you personally, and why?
2. How does the father's response to his wayward son challenge our understanding of God's love and forgiveness?
3. In what ways do we see ourselves reflected in the characters of the prodigal son, the older brother, or the loving father?
4. What lessons can we learn from the father's example of unconditional love and forgiveness, and how can we apply these principles in our relationships with others?
5. How does the parable of the Prodigal Son remind us of the depth of God's love for us, his willingness to forgive our sins, and his desire for reconciliation and restoration in our lives?

Lesson 16

The Crucifixion and Resurrection: The Foundation of Christian Faith

Scripture: Matthew 27:32-66, Matthew 28:1-10
- 1 Corinthians 15:3-8

Memory Verse
- 1 Corinthians 15:3-4 - "For what I received I passed on to you as of first importance: that Christ died for our sins according to the Scriptures, that he was buried, that he was raised on the third day according to the Scriptures."

Exposition

The crucifixion and resurrection of Jesus Christ are central to the Christian faith, serving as the foundation of our hope, redemption, and eternal life. Through his sacrificial death on the cross, Jesus atoned for the sins of humanity, offering forgiveness and reconciliation to all who would believe in him. And through his victorious resurrection from the dead, Jesus conquered sin, death, and the powers of darkness, securing for us the promise of new life and eternal salvation.

As we reflect on the events of Jesus' crucifixion, we are confronted with the harsh reality of human sin and rebellion against God. Yet, in the midst of our brokenness and shame, we find hope and redemption in the outstretched arms of Jesus on the cross, who bore our sins and suffered in our place. And as we celebrate his resurrection from the dead, we are reminded of the power of God to overcome sin and death, and the assurance of our own resurrection to eternal life through faith in Christ.

Discuss Questions

1. Why is the crucifixion and resurrection of Jesus Christ considered the foundation of the Christian faith?
2. How do the events of Jesus' crucifixion and resurrection fulfill the Old Testament prophecies and promises concerning the Messiah and Savior of the world?
3. What significance do the cross and the empty tomb hold for believers in terms of forgiveness, redemption, and new life in Christ?
4. In what ways does the crucifixion and resurrection of Jesus Christ offer hope and assurance to believers in the face of suffering, sin, and death?
5. How does the message of the crucifixion and resurrection challenge us to live lives of faith, obedience, and hope in the midst of a broken and fallen world?

Lesson 17

Prayer: Connecting with God Daily

Scripture: Matthew 6:5-15, Philippians 4:6-7, 1 Thessalonians 5:16-18

Memory Verse
- Philippians 4:6 - "Do not be anxious about anything, but in every situation, by prayer and petition, with thanksgiving, present your requests to God."

Exposition

Prayer is a vital aspect of the Christian life, serving as a means of communication, communion, and connection with God. Through prayer, we express our adoration, confession, thanksgiving, and supplication to our Heavenly Father, drawing near to him with confidence and trust in his goodness and faithfulness. As Jesus taught his disciples, prayer is not merely a religious duty or ritual, but a relational encounter with the living God, who delights in hearing and answering the prayers of his children.

In this lesson, we will explore the significance of prayer in the life of a believer, the various forms and expressions of prayer, and practical strategies for cultivating a vibrant and consistent prayer life. Through prayer, we have the privilege of experiencing the presence, peace, and power of God in our lives, as we entrust our cares, concerns, and desires into his loving hands.

Discussion Questions

1. Why is prayer important in the life of a believer, and how does it deepen our relationship with God?
2. What are some of the different types of prayer mentioned in Scripture, and how can we incorporate them into our daily lives?
3. What challenges or obstacles do you face in maintaining a consistent prayer life, and how can you overcome them?
4. How have you experienced the faithfulness of God in answering prayer, and what role does trust play in our prayer life?
5. What practical steps can you take to deepen your prayer life and cultivate a closer walk with God on a daily basis?

Lesson 18

Bible Study: Digging Deeper into God's Word

Scripture: 2 Timothy 3:16-17, Psalm 119:105, Hebrews 4:12

Memory Verse
- Psalm 119:105 - "Your word is a lamp for my feet, a light on my path."

Exposition

Bible study is essential for spiritual growth and maturity, as it allows us to immerse ourselves in the living Word of God, which is living and active, sharper than any two-edged sword. Through the study of Scripture, we gain insight into God's character, his will for our lives, and his redemptive plan for humanity. As disciples of Christ, we are called to be diligent students of the Word, rightly handling the word of truth and allowing it to transform our hearts and minds.

In this lesson, we will explore the importance of Bible study in the life of a believer, the principles and methods of effective Bible study, and practical strategies for engaging with God's Word on a deeper level. Through regular study and meditation on Scripture, we can grow in knowledge, wisdom, and understanding, and be equipped for every good work that God has prepared for us.

Discussion Questions

1. Why is Bible study important for spiritual growth and maturity, and how does it deepen our understanding of God and his purposes?
2. What are some practical strategies for approaching Bible study, such as choosing a passage, asking questions, and applying the truths learned?
3. How does the Holy Spirit illuminate Scripture and guide us into all truth as we study God's Word?
4. What role does prayer play in Bible study, and how can we invite the Holy Spirit to speak to us through Scripture?

Lesson 19

Worship: Expressing Love and Gratitude to God

Scripture: Psalm 95:1-7, John 4:23-24, Hebrews 12:28-29

Memory Verse
- Psalm 95:1 - "Come, let us sing for joy to the Lord; let us shout aloud to the Rock of our salvation."

Exposition

Worship is more than just singing songs or attending church services; it is an expression of love, adoration, and gratitude towards God for who he is and what he has done. In Scripture, we are commanded to worship the Lord with gladness, to come into his presence with singing, and to give thanks to him and praise his name. Through worship, we declare God's worthiness, proclaim his glory, and surrender our lives to his lordship and sovereignty.

In this lesson, we will explore the biblical principles of worship, the various forms and expressions of worship, and the transformative power of worship in the life of a believer. Whether through music, prayer, Scripture reading, or acts of service, worship is an opportunity to encounter the presence of God, to draw near to him with reverence and awe, and to offer ourselves as living sacrifices, holy and pleasing to God.

Discussion Questions

1. What does it mean to worship God in spirit and in truth, and how does worship deepen our relationship with him?
2. What are some of the different ways that worship is expressed in Scripture, and how can we incorporate these elements into our corporate and personal worship experiences?
3. How does worship impact our perspective on God, ourselves, and the world around us, and how can it shape our attitudes and actions?
4. In what ways does worship foster unity and community among believers, as we gather together to exalt the name of Jesus?

Lesson 20

Service: Putting Faith into Action through Acts of Kindness

Scripture: Matthew 25:31-46, Galatians 5:13-14, James 2:14-17

Memory Verse
- Galatians 5:13 - "For you were called to freedom, brothers. Only do not use your freedom as an opportunity for the flesh, but through love serve one another."

Exposition

Service is a tangible expression of our faith in action, as we demonstrate the love of Christ through acts of kindness, compassion, and selflessness towards others. Throughout Scripture, we are called to serve one another in love, using our gifts, talents, and resources to meet the needs of those around us and to advance God's kingdom on earth. As followers of Jesus, we are called to follow his example of humble service, as he came not to be served, but to serve, and to give his life as a ransom for many.

In this lesson, we will explore the biblical principles of service, the various opportunities for service within the church and the community, and the transformative impact of service on both the servant and the recipient. Through acts of kindness, mercy, and justice, we have the privilege of being the hands and feet of Jesus in the world, bringing hope, healing, and restoration to those in need.

Discussion Questions

1. How does the example of Jesus Christ inspire and challenge us to serve others with humility, compassion, and selflessness?
2. What are some practical ways that we can demonstrate love and kindness through acts of service in our local church, community, and beyond?
3. How does engaging in acts of service impact our spiritual growth, deepen our relationships with others, and reflect the character of God to the world around us?

Lesson 21

Fellowship: Building Strong Relationships within the Church Community

Scripture: Acts 2:42-47, Hebrews 10:24-25, 1 Thessalonians 5:11

Memory Verse
- Acts 2:42 - "And they devoted themselves to the apostles' teaching and the fellowship, to the breaking of bread and the prayers."

Exposition

Fellowship is an essential aspect of the Christian life, as we are called to live in community with one another, encouraging, supporting, and building each other up in faith and love. In the early church, believers devoted themselves to fellowship, gathering together regularly for worship, prayer, teaching, and the breaking of bread. Through their shared life and unity of purpose, they experienced the transformative power of community and became a living testimony to the love and grace of God.

In this lesson, we will explore the importance of fellowship in the life of the church, the characteristics of biblical fellowship, and practical ways to cultivate strong relationships within the church community. By prioritizing fellowship and investing in authentic relationships, we strengthen the bonds of unity, build resilience in times of trial, and bear witness to the transformative power of God's love in our lives.

Discussion Questions

1. Why is fellowship important for spiritual growth and maturity, and how does it strengthen our relationship with God and with one another?
2. What are some of the characteristics of biblical fellowship, as demonstrated by the early church in Acts 2:42-47?
3. How can we foster a culture of genuine fellowship within our church community, where believers feel welcomed, valued, and supported in their journey of faith?

Lesson 22

Evangelism: Sharing the Good News with Others

Scripture: Matthew 28:18-20, Acts 1:8, Romans 10:14-15

Memory Verse
- Matthew 28:19 - "Go therefore and make disciples of all nations, baptizing them in the name of the Father and of the Son and of the Holy Spirit."

Exposition

Evangelism is the proclamation of the gospel message and the invitation for others to respond to the saving grace of Jesus Christ. As disciples of Jesus, we are called to be ambassadors of reconciliation, sharing the good news of salvation with those who have not yet heard or believed. Through our words, actions, and lifestyle, we bear witness to the love and truth of Christ, compelling others to repentance and faith.

In this lesson, we will explore the biblical mandate for evangelism, the urgency of sharing the gospel message, and practical strategies for engaging in evangelistic outreach. By being intentional and bold in our witness, we participate in God's redemptive work in the world, bringing hope, healing, and salvation to those who are lost and searching for meaning and purpose in life.

Discussion Questions

1. Why is evangelism essential for fulfilling the Great Commission and advancing God's kingdom on earth?

2. What are some of the barriers or obstacles that prevent believers from engaging in evangelistic outreach, and how can we overcome them?

3. How can we effectively share the gospel message with others in our context, meeting them where they are and addressing their spiritual needs with sensitivity and compassion?

Lesson 23

Identity and Self-Worth in Christ

Scripture: Genesis 1:27, Ephesians 2:10, 1 Peter 2:9

Memory Verse
- Ephesians 2:10 - "For we are God's handiwork, created in Christ Jesus to do good works, which God prepared in advance for us to do."

Exposition

Our identity and self-worth are deeply rooted in our relationship with Jesus Christ, who has redeemed us and called us his own. In a world that often defines worth by external factors such as appearance, achievements, or popularity, our true value comes from being created in the image of God and being adopted into his family through faith in Christ. Understanding and embracing our identity in Christ empowers us to live with confidence, purpose, and dignity, knowing that we are loved, accepted, and cherished by our Heavenly Father.

In this lesson, we will explore the biblical truths about identity and self-worth, the significance of being children of God, and practical ways to cultivate a healthy sense of identity grounded in Christ. By anchoring our identity in the unchanging love and acceptance of God, we can withstand the pressures and expectations of the world and live with authenticity, joy, and purpose.

Discussion Questions

1. How does understanding our identity in Christ impact our sense of self-worth and value?
2. What are some common misconceptions or false sources of identity and self-worth in today's culture, and how do they compare to the biblical perspective?
3. What practical steps can we take to cultivate a healthy sense of identity in Christ, rooted in the truth of God's Word and his love for us?

Lesson 24

Relationships: Honoring God in Friendships and Dating

Scripture: Proverbs 13:20, 1 Corinthians 15:33, 2 Corinthians 6:14

Memory Verse
- Proverbs 13:20 - "Walk with the wise and become wise, for a companion of fools suffers harm."

Exposition

Our relationships play a significant role in shaping our character, values, and spiritual growth. As followers of Christ, we are called to honor God in all of our relationships, whether with friends, family members, or romantic partners. This involves choosing companions who share our faith and values, treating others with love and respect, and seeking relationships that encourage us to grow closer to God and live according to his Word. By building healthy and godly relationships, we reflect the love of Christ to the world and experience the blessings of fellowship and community.

In this lesson, we will explore the biblical principles of friendship and dating, the qualities of healthy relationships, and practical guidelines for honoring God in our interactions with others. By seeking wisdom and guidance from Scripture, we can navigate the complexities of relationships with integrity, discernment, and grace, seeking to glorify God in all that we do.

Discussion Questions

1. How do our relationships with others impact our spiritual growth and walk with God?

2. What are some biblical principles for building healthy and godly friendships and dating relationships?

3. How can we discern God's guidance and will for our relationships, and what role does prayer and seeking wise counsel play in this process?

Lesson 25

Peer Pressure: Standing Firm in Faith

Scripture: Proverbs 1:10, Romans 12:2
- 1 Peter 4:12-16

Memory Verse
- Romans 12:2 - "Do not conform to the pattern of this world, but be transformed by the renewing of your mind. Then you will be able to test and approve what God's will is—his good, pleasing and perfect will."

Exposition

Peer pressure is a powerful influence that can shape our beliefs, behaviors, and choices, often leading us away from God's truth and will for our lives. As young Christians, we are called to stand firm in our faith and resist the pressures to conform to the values and standards of the world. This requires courage, discernment, and a commitment to living according to God's Word, even when it means standing alone or facing opposition from others. By anchoring ourselves in Christ and surrounding ourselves with supportive and like-minded believers, we can withstand the pressures of peer influence and live as lights in a dark world.

In this lesson, we will explore the challenges of peer pressure, the importance of standing firm in our faith, and practical strategies for resisting negative influences and living with integrity and conviction. By relying on the strength and guidance of the Holy Spirit, we can navigate the complexities of peer relationships with wisdom, courage, and grace, remaining steadfast in our commitment to follow Jesus Christ.

Discussion Questions

1. How does peer pressure influence our beliefs, behaviors, and choices, and what are some common examples of peer pressure in today's culture?
2. What does it mean to stand firm in our faith, and how can we resist the pressures to conform to the values and standards of the world?
3. What practical steps can we take to strengthen our resolve and remain steadfast in our commitment to follow Jesus Christ, even in the face of opposition or ridicule from others?

Lesson 26

Handling Stress and Anxiety God's Way

Scripture: Philippians 4:6-7, Matthew 11:28-30, 1 Peter 5:7

Memory Verse
- Philippians 4:6 - "Do not be anxious about anything, but in every situation, by prayer and petition, with thanksgiving, present your requests to God."

Exposition

In today's fast-paced and demanding world, stress and anxiety have become prevalent issues that many people struggle with, including teenagers. As Christians, we are not immune to the pressures and challenges of life, but we have the assurance that God offers us peace and comfort in the midst of our struggles. Through prayer, trust, and reliance on God's strength, we can overcome stress and anxiety and experience the peace that surpasses all understanding.

In this lesson, we will explore biblical principles for handling stress and anxiety, practical strategies for managing our emotions and thoughts, and the importance of seeking help and support from trusted mentors and counselors. By casting our cares on the Lord and trusting in his provision, we can find rest for our souls and strength for the journey ahead.

Discussion Questions

1. What are some common sources of stress and anxiety in your life, and how do they affect your physical, emotional, and spiritual well-being?
2. How does the Bible encourage us to respond to stress and anxiety, and what are some practical strategies for applying these principles in your daily life?
3. In what ways can prayer, meditation on Scripture, and seeking support from trusted friends and mentors help us cope with stress and anxiety and experience God's peace?

Lesson 27

Social Media and Technology: Navigating the Digital World with Wisdom

Scripture: Psalm 101:3, Ephesians 5:15-16, 1 Corinthians 10:31

Memory Verse
- Psalm 101:3 - "I will not look with approval on anything that is vile. I hate what faithless people do; I will have no part in it."

Exposition

Social media and technology have revolutionized the way we communicate, connect, and engage with the world around us. While these tools offer many benefits and opportunities for learning and collaboration, they also present unique challenges and dangers, particularly for young people. As Christians, we are called to exercise wisdom and discernment in our use of social media and technology, being mindful of their potential impact on our relationships, mental health, and spiritual growth.

In this lesson, we will explore biblical principles for navigating the digital world with wisdom and integrity, practical guidelines for using social media and technology responsibly, and the importance of maintaining healthy boundaries and habits. By honoring God with our online presence and using technology as a tool for good, we can be salt and light in the digital age, shining the love and truth of Christ in all that we do.

Discussion Questions

1. What are some of the positive and negative aspects of social media and technology in your life, and how do they impact your relationships, mental health, and spiritual well-being?
2. How can we honor God with our online presence and use social media and technology as tools for good and positive influence?
3. What are some practical strategies for maintaining healthy boundaries and habits in our use of social media and technology, and how can we avoid the pitfalls of comparison, distraction, and addiction?

Lesson 28

Bullying and Conflict Resolution: Responding with Grace and Forgiveness

Scripture: Matthew 5:38-39, Romans 12:17-21, Ephesians 4:31-32

Memory Verse
- Ephesians 4:32 - "Be kind to one another, tenderhearted, forgiving one another, as God in Christ forgave you."

Exposition

Bullying and conflict are unfortunate realities that many teenagers face in their daily lives, whether at school, in their communities, or even within their own families. As followers of Christ, we are called to respond to these challenges with grace, love, and forgiveness, following the example of Jesus who taught us to turn the other cheek and to overcome evil with good. By addressing conflict with humility, empathy, and a commitment to reconciliation, we can break the cycle of violence and build a culture of peace and understanding.

In this lesson, we will explore biblical principles for responding to bullying and conflict with grace and forgiveness, practical strategies for resolving conflicts peacefully, and the importance of seeking support and intervention when necessary. By extending grace and forgiveness to those who have wronged us, we demonstrate the transformative power of God's love and mercy, and pave the way for healing and reconciliation in our relationships.

Discussion Questions

1. How have you or someone you know been affected by bullying or conflict, and what were some of the challenges or emotions you experienced as a result?
2. What does it mean to respond to bullying and conflict with grace and forgiveness, and how does this reflect the character of Christ?
3. How can we effectively resolve conflicts and address bullying in our schools, communities, and churches, and what role can we play in promoting a culture of peace and understanding?

Lesson 29

Mental Health Awareness: Finding Hope and Healing in Christ

Scripture: Psalm 34:17-18, Isaiah 41:10, 2 Corinthians 1:3-4

Memory Verse
- Psalm 34:18 - "The Lord is close to the brokenhearted and saves those who are crushed in spirit."

Exposition

Mental health is a significant issue that affects millions of people worldwide, including teenagers who may struggle with anxiety, depression, self-esteem issues, and other mental health challenges. As Christians, we believe that our hope and healing ultimately come from God, who is our refuge and strength in times of trouble. Through prayer, community support, and professional intervention, we can find comfort, strength, and restoration in Christ, who understands our pain and offers us the promise of peace and wholeness.

In this lesson, we will explore the importance of mental health awareness, the biblical perspective on suffering and healing, and practical steps for finding hope and support in Christ. By breaking the stigma surrounding mental illness and reaching out to those who are struggling, we can create a safe and supportive environment where everyone feels valued, accepted, and loved.

Discussion Questions

1. What are some common misconceptions or stigmas associated with mental illness, and how do they impact individuals who are struggling with mental health challenges?
2. How does the Bible offer hope and comfort to those who are experiencing emotional or psychological pain, and what are some practical ways we can support and encourage one another in times of struggle?
3. What resources and support systems are available for teenagers who are struggling with mental health issues, and how can we promote mental health awareness and advocacy within our communities and churches?

Lesson 30

Social Justice: Advocating for Equality and Compassion

Scripture: Micah 6:8, Isaiah 1:17 Galatians 3:28

Memory Verse
- Micah 6:8 - "He has shown you, O mortal, what is good. And what does the Lord require of you? To act justly and to love mercy and to walk humbly with your God."

Exposition

Social justice is a central theme in the Bible, as God calls us to uphold the dignity and rights of all people, particularly the marginalized and oppressed. As followers of Christ, we are called to be agents of change in a world marked by injustice, inequality, and suffering, advocating for equality, compassion, and the rights of the vulnerable. Through acts of kindness, advocacy, and empowerment, we can make a difference in the lives of those who are marginalized and work towards building a more just and compassionate society.

In this lesson, we will explore biblical principles for social justice, the importance of standing up for the rights of others, and practical ways to advocate for equality and compassion in our communities and beyond. By aligning our hearts with God's heart for justice and mercy, we can be a voice for the voiceless and a light in the darkness, bringing hope and healing to a broken world.

Discussion Questions

1. What does it mean to pursue social justice, and why is it important for Christians to advocate for equality and compassion?
2. How do the teachings of Jesus and the prophets inspire us to seek justice, love mercy, and walk humbly with God?
3. What are some practical ways we can address issues of injustice and inequality in our communities, such as poverty, racism, and human trafficking, and how can we make a difference in the lives of those who are marginalized or oppressed?

Lesson 31

Environmental Stewardship: Caring for God's Creation

Scripture: Genesis 2:15, Psalm 24:1-2, Romans 8:19-21

Memory Verse
- Genesis 2:15 - "The Lord God took the man and put him in the Garden of Eden to work it and take care of it."

Exposition

Environmental stewardship is a biblical mandate that calls us to care for God's creation and to be responsible stewards of the earth and its resources. As Christians, we believe that the earth is the Lord's and everything in it, and that we are called to exercise wise and compassionate stewardship over the environment for the glory of God and the well-being of future generations. By adopting sustainable practices, reducing our carbon footprint, and advocating for policies that protect the environment, we can fulfill our God-given mandate to care for creation and to be good stewards of the earth.

In this lesson, we will explore the biblical basis for environmental stewardship, the current challenges facing our planet, and practical steps for caring for God's creation. By cultivating a deeper appreciation for the beauty and diversity of the natural world, we can become more mindful of our impact on the environment and take meaningful action to preserve and protect God's creation for generations to come.

Discussion Questions

1. Why is environmental stewardship important for Christians, and how does caring for God's creation reflect our love for God and our neighbors?
2. What are some of the current environmental challenges facing our planet, and how do they impact ecosystems, wildlife, and human communities?
3. What are some practical ways we can practice environmental stewardship in our daily lives, such as reducing waste, conserving energy, and supporting conservation efforts, and how can we advocate for policies that protect the environment?

Lesson 32

Substance Abuse and Addiction: Choosing God's Path to Freedom

Scripture: Galatians 5:1, Romans 6:14, 1 Corinthians 10:13

Memory Verse
- Galatians 5:1 - "It is for freedom that Christ has set us free. Stand firm, then, and do not let yourselves be burdened again by a yoke of slavery."

Exposition

Substance abuse and addiction are complex issues that affect individuals and families in profound ways, often leading to brokenness, despair, and loss. As followers of Christ, we believe that true freedom and healing are found in Jesus Christ, who offers us hope, forgiveness, and the power to overcome the chains of addiction. By surrendering our struggles to God, seeking support from trusted mentors and counselors, and walking in obedience to his Word, we can experience the transformative power of God's grace and find the path to lasting freedom and recovery.

In this lesson, we will explore the biblical perspective on addiction and recovery, the importance of seeking help and support, and practical steps for overcoming substance abuse and addiction. By embracing the truth of God's Word and relying on the strength of the Holy Spirit, we can break free from the bondage of addiction and walk in the freedom and victory that Christ has won for us.

Discussion Questions

1. How does addiction impact individuals and families, and what are some of the root causes and triggers that contribute to substance abuse?

2. What does the Bible teach us about addiction and recovery, and how can we find hope and healing in Christ?

3. What are some practical steps we can take to overcome substance abuse and addiction, such as seeking professional help, accountability, and support groups, and how can we support those who are struggling with addiction in our communities and churches?

Lesson 33

Sexual Purity and Integrity: God's Design for Holiness

Scripture: 1 Thessalonians 4:3-5, Ephesians 5:3-5, Matthew 5:27-28

Memory Verse
- 1 Thessalonians 4:3 - "For this is the will of God, your sanctification: that you abstain from sexual immorality."

Exposition

Sexual purity and integrity are essential aspects of the Christian life, as God calls us to honor our bodies and our relationships according to his design and purpose. In a culture that often promotes promiscuity, pornography, and other forms of sexual immorality, we are called to stand firm in our commitment to purity, recognizing that our bodies are temples of the Holy Spirit and that sexual intimacy is a sacred gift from God to be cherished and protected. By cultivating a lifestyle of holiness and integrity, we honor God, protect ourselves from harm, and experience the fullness of his blessings in our lives.

In this lesson, we will explore the biblical principles for sexual purity and integrity, the consequences of sexual immorality, and practical strategies for guarding our hearts and minds against temptation. By submitting our desires and impulses to the lordship of Christ, we can walk in purity and holiness, living as lights in a dark and broken world.

Discussion Questions

1. Why is sexual purity important for Christians, and how does it reflect our commitment to holiness and obedience to God's Word?
2. What are some of the challenges and temptations that young people face in maintaining sexual purity, and how can we overcome them with the help of the Holy Spirit?
3. What are some practical steps we can take to guard our hearts and minds against sexual immorality, such as setting boundaries, seeking accountability, and renewing our minds with God's Word?

Lesson 34

Cultural Diversity: Embracing God's Beautiful creation of Humanity

Scripture: Revelation 7:9-10, Galatians 3:28, Acts 17:26-27

Memory Verse
- Revelation 7:9 - "After this I looked, and behold, a great multitude that no one could number, from every nation, from all tribes and peoples and languages, standing before the throne and before the Lamb, clothed in white robes, with palm branches in their hands."

Exposition

Cultural diversity is a reflection of God's creativity and sovereignty, as he has created people from every nation, tribe, and tongue to bear his image and reflect his glory. As Christians, we are called to embrace and celebrate the rich nature of humanity, recognizing that every person is created in the image of God and worthy of love, respect, and dignity. By breaking down barriers of prejudice and discrimination, we can build bridges of understanding and unity, fostering a community where all are valued and welcomed as cherished members of God's family.

In this lesson, we will explore the biblical perspective on cultural diversity, the beauty of God's diverse creation, and practical ways to embrace and celebrate diversity in our communities and churches. By seeking to understand and appreciate the unique contributions of different cultures and ethnicities, we can build relationships that reflect the love and unity of Christ, and bear witness to the transforming power of the gospel.

Discussion Questions

1. Why is cultural diversity important for Christians, and how does it enrich our understanding of God and his kingdom?
2. What are some of the barriers and challenges to embracing cultural diversity, and how can we overcome them through humility, empathy, and love?
3. How can we celebrate and honor the diversity of cultures and ethnicities in our communities and churches, and what role can we play in promoting reconciliation and unity in a divided world?

Lesson 35

Discipleship: Following Jesus' Example in Everyday Life

Scripture: Matthew 16:24, Luke 9:23, John 13:15

Memory Verse
- Matthew 16:24 - "Then Jesus said to his disciples, 'If anyone would come after me, let him deny himself and take up his cross and follow me.'"

Exposition

Discipleship is the lifelong journey of following Jesus Christ, learning from his teachings, and imitating his example in every area of our lives. As disciples of Jesus, we are called to surrender our wills, take up our cross, and follow him wholeheartedly, embracing his values, priorities, and mission. Through intimate fellowship with Christ, obedience to his Word, and service to others, we grow in our likeness to him and become effective witnesses of his love and grace to the world.

In this lesson, we will explore the meaning and significance of discipleship, the cost of following Jesus, and practical ways to live out our faith in everyday life. By cultivating a lifestyle of discipleship, we can experience the joy of knowing Christ intimately, the power of his resurrection, and the fulfillment of his purpose for our lives.

Discussion Questions

1. What does it mean to be a disciple of Jesus, and how does discipleship shape our identity, values, and priorities?
2. What are some of the challenges and sacrifices involved in following Jesus, and how can we overcome them with the help of the Holy Spirit?
3. What are some practical ways we can live out our faith in everyday life, such as prayer, study of Scripture, fellowship with believers, and acts of service, and how do these practices deepen our discipleship journey?

Lesson 36

Spiritual Disciplines: Cultivating a Vibrant Relationship with God

Scripture: 1 Timothy 4:7-8, Psalm 119:11, James 4:8

Memory Verse
- Psalm 119:11 - "I have hidden your word in my heart that I might not sin against you."

Exposition

Spiritual disciplines are intentional practices that cultivate a vibrant and intimate relationship with God, enabling us to grow in our faith, deepen our knowledge of his Word, and experience the power of his presence in our lives. As followers of Christ, we are called to engage in disciplines such as prayer, meditation, fasting, study of Scripture, worship, and service, as means of grace that draw us closer to God and transform us into his likeness. Through consistent practice and reliance on the Holy Spirit, we can experience spiritual growth, renewal, and transformation in our lives.

In this lesson, we will explore the importance and benefits of spiritual disciplines, practical strategies for incorporating them into our daily routines, and the role of discipline in deepening our relationship with God. By prioritizing intimacy with God and making space for him in our lives, we can experience the fullness of his love, power, and presence, and become more effective disciples and witnesses of his kingdom.

Discussion Questions

1. What are spiritual disciplines, and why are they important for nurturing our relationship with God and fostering spiritual growth?
2. What are some of the key spiritual disciplines practiced by Jesus and the early church, and how can we emulate their example in our own lives?
3. How can we overcome obstacles and distractions to practicing spiritual disciplines, and what are some practical steps we can take to cultivate a consistent and vibrant spiritual life?

Lesson 37

Forgiveness: Extending Grace as Christ Has Forgiven Us

Scriptures: Ephesians 4:32, Colossians 3:13, Matthew 6:14-15

Memory Verse
- Ephesians 4:32 - "Be kind to one another, tenderhearted, forgiving one another, as God in Christ forgave you."

Exposition

Forgiveness is at the heart of the Christian faith, as we have been forgiven by God through the sacrifice of Jesus Christ and are called to extend that same grace and mercy to others. As followers of Christ, we are called to forgive those who have wronged us, release them from the debt of their sin, and reconcile with them in love and humility. Through forgiveness, we experience the freedom and healing that comes from letting go of bitterness and resentment, and we reflect the character of Christ to the world.

In this lesson, we will explore the biblical principles of forgiveness, the benefits of extending grace to others, and practical steps for forgiving those who have hurt us. By following the example of Jesus, who forgave his enemies even as he hung on the cross, we can experience the power of forgiveness to heal relationships, restore brokenness, and bring reconciliation and peace.

Discussion Questions

1. Why is forgiveness important for Christians, and how does it reflect the grace and mercy of God?
2. What are some of the barriers or obstacles to forgiveness, and how can we overcome them with the help of the Holy Spirit?
3. What are some practical steps we can take to forgive those who have wronged us, such as prayer, seeking reconciliation, and extending grace, and how does forgiveness lead to healing and restoration in relationships?

Lesson 38

Leadership: Using Your Gifts to Serve Others

Scripture: Romans 12:6-8, 1 Peter 4:10-11, Matthew 20:26-28

Memory Verse
- 1 Peter 4:10 - "Each of you should use whatever gift you have received to serve others, as faithful stewards of God's grace in its various forms."

Exposition

Leadership is not about asserting authority or seeking recognition, but rather about using our God-given gifts and abilities to serve others and advance God's kingdom purposes. As Christians, we are called to lead by example, following the servant-hearted example of Jesus Christ who came not to be served, but to serve and to give his life as a ransom for many. Whether in our families, communities, schools, or churches, we have the opportunity to lead with humility, integrity, and love, inspiring and empowering others to fulfill their God-given potential and to make a positive impact in the world.

In this lesson, we will explore the biblical principles of servant leadership, the qualities of effective leadership, and practical strategies for using our gifts to serve others. By embracing our role as stewards of God's grace and investing our time, talents, and resources in the service of others, we can lead with humility and purpose, and leave a lasting legacy of love and impact.

Discussion Questions

1. What is the biblical concept of servant leadership, and how does it differ from worldly notions of leadership?
2. What are some examples of servant leadership in the Bible, and how do they inspire and challenge us to lead with humility and compassion?
3. How can we identify and develop our leadership gifts and talents, and what are some practical ways we can use them to serve others and make a positive difference in our communities and beyond?

Lesson 39

Decision Making: Seeking God's Will in Every Choice

Scripture: Proverbs 3:5-6, James 1:5, Romans 12:2

Memory Verse
- Proverbs 3:5-6 - "Trust in the Lord with all your heart and lean not on your own understanding; in all your ways submit to him, and he will make your paths straight."

Exposition

Decision making is a fundamental aspect of life, as we are constantly faced with choices that shape our actions, relationships, and future. As Christians, we are called to seek God's will and guidance in every decision we make, trusting in his wisdom, sovereignty, and love to lead us in the right path. By aligning our desires and decisions with God's Word and his purposes, we can experience the peace, direction, and fulfillment that come from walking in obedience to his will.

In this lesson, we will explore the biblical principles of decision making, the importance of seeking God's guidance, and practical strategies for discerning his will in every choice. By cultivating a lifestyle of prayer, surrender, and obedience, we can make decisions with confidence, knowing that God is leading us and working all things together for our good and his glory.

Discussion Questions

1. Why is it important for Christians to seek God's will in their decision making, and how does it reflect our trust and dependence on him?
2. What are some common challenges or obstacles to discerning God's will, and how can we overcome them with the help of the Holy Spirit and wise counsel?
3. What are some practical steps we can take to discern God's will in our decision making, such as prayer, studying Scripture, seeking wise counsel, and listening to the promptings of the Holy Spirit, and how can we trust in God's providence and faithfulness as we navigate life's choices and challenges?

Lesson 40

Education and Career: Honoring God in Your Vocational Calling

Scripture: Colossians 3:23-24, Proverbs 16:3, Ephesians 4:1

Memory Verse
- **Colossians 3:23** - "Whatever you do, work at it with all your heart, as working for the Lord, not for human masters."

Exposition

Education and career are important aspects of life that provide opportunities for personal growth, fulfillment, and service to others. As Christians, we are called to approach our educational and vocational pursuits with excellence, integrity, and a desire to glorify God in all that we do. Whether we are students, employees, entrepreneurs, or homemakers, we have the privilege and responsibility to use our talents and abilities to make a positive impact in the world and to advance God's kingdom purposes.

In this lesson, we will explore the biblical principles of vocational calling, the importance of using our gifts and talents for God's glory, and practical strategies for pursuing education and career paths that align with God's purposes for our lives. By seeking God's guidance and wisdom in our vocational decisions, we can find fulfillment and purpose in our work, and make a meaningful contribution to the world around us.

Discussion Questions

1. How does your education or career path align with your understanding of God's calling for your life, and how do you seek to honor God in your vocational pursuits?

2. What are some biblical examples of individuals who used their skills and talents to serve God in their professions, and how can we emulate their example in our own lives?

3. What are some practical ways we can integrate our faith into our education and career choices, such as seeking opportunities for service, maintaining integrity in the workplace, and using our resources to bless others?

Lesson 41

Financial Stewardship: Managing Resources Wisely for God's Kingdom

Scripture: Matthew 6:19-21, Proverbs 3:9-10, Luke 16:10-11

Memory Verse
- Matthew 6:21 - "For where your treasure is, there your heart will be also."

Exposition

Financial stewardship is a vital aspect of the Christian life, as we are called to manage our resources wisely and generously for the glory of God and the advancement of his kingdom. As stewards of God's blessings, we are called to honor him with our finances, to live within our means, to give generously to those in need, and to invest in kingdom priorities that align with God's values and purposes. By cultivating a heart of gratitude, generosity, and faithfulness in our financial stewardship, we can experience the joy of participating in God's work and making an eternal impact in the lives of others.

In this lesson, we will explore the biblical principles of financial stewardship, the importance of budgeting, saving, giving, and investing, and practical strategies for managing our finances in a way that honors God and blesses others. By seeking first God's kingdom and righteousness in our financial decisions, we can experience the peace and provision that come from trusting in his faithfulness and generosity.

Discussion Questions

1. How do you view money and possessions in light of your faith, and how do your financial decisions reflect your commitment to honoring God with your resources?
2. What are some biblical principles of financial stewardship, such as giving generously, living within your means, and avoiding debt, and how do they apply to your life?
3. What are some practical steps you can take to manage your finances wisely and align your spending, saving, giving, and investing with God's kingdom purposes, and how can you use your resources to bless others and advance God's work in the world?

Lesson 42

Family Values: Building Strong Foundations for Future Relationships

Scripture: Psalm 127:3-5, Ephesians 5:22-6:4, Proverbs 22:6

Memory Verse
- Psalm 127:1a - "Unless the Lord builds the house, the builders labor in vain."

Exposition

Family is the cornerstone of society, and strong family values are essential for building healthy relationships, nurturing children, and fostering a culture of love and respect. As Christians, we are called to prioritize our relationships with God and with our families, cultivating environments of love, grace, and unity that reflect God's heart for his people. By modeling Christ-like character and values in our homes, teaching our children to love and serve others, and investing time and resources in building strong family bonds, we can lay a firm foundation for future generations and leave a legacy of faith that endures.

In this lesson, we will explore the importance of family values, the biblical principles of marriage and parenting, and practical strategies for building strong foundations for future relationships. By committing our families to the Lord and seeking his wisdom and guidance in our roles as spouses, parents, and children, we can experience the joy and fulfillment of family life as God intended.

Discussion Questions

1. What are some of the core values and priorities that shape your family life, and how do they reflect your commitment to following Christ?

2. What does the Bible teach us about marriage, parenting, and the roles and responsibilities of family members, and how can we apply these principles in our own families?

3. What are some practical ways we can strengthen our family relationships and cultivate an environment of love, grace, and unity in our homes, and how can we pass on our faith and values to the next generation?

Lesson 43

Mission and Purpose: Discovering Your Unique Calling in God's Kingdom

Scripture: Jeremiah 29:11, Ephesians 2:10, Romans 12:4-8

Memory Verse
- Jeremiah 29:11 - "For I know the plans I have for you," declares the Lord, "plans to prosper you and not to harm you, plans to give you hope and a future."

Exposition

Understanding our mission and purpose in life is essential for living a fulfilling and impactful life as a follower of Christ. Each of us is uniquely created by God with specific gifts, talents, and passions to contribute to his kingdom work. Discovering and embracing our calling involves seeking God's guidance, discerning our strengths and weaknesses, and being willing to step out in faith to fulfill the purposes for which we were created. By aligning our lives with God's will and walking in obedience to his leading, we can experience the joy and fulfillment of fulfilling our mission and purpose in his kingdom.

In this lesson, we will explore the biblical principles of mission and purpose, the importance of discovering and embracing our unique calling, and practical strategies for discerning God's will for our lives. By seeking first God's kingdom and righteousness and surrendering our plans and desires to him, we can experience the abundant life and fulfillment that come from walking in alignment with his purposes.

Discussion Questions

1. How do you define mission and purpose, and why is it important for Christians to discover and embrace their unique calling in God's kingdom?
2. What are some biblical examples of individuals who discovered and fulfilled their God-given mission and purpose, and how can we apply their lessons to our own lives?
3. What are some practical steps we can take to discern God's will and calling for our lives, such as prayer, seeking wise counsel, and stepping out in faith, and how can we overcome obstacles and doubts to fully embrace our mission and purpose in Christ?

Lesson 44

Vision and Goals: Pursuing God's Dreams for Your Life

Scripture: Habakkuk 2:2-3, Proverbs 29:18, Philippians 3:13-14

Memory Verse
- Habakkuk 2:2 - "Then the Lord replied: "Write down the revelation and make it plain on tablets so that a herald may run with it."

Exposition

Having a clear vision and setting goals are essential for living with intentionality and purpose, both personally and spiritually. God has dreams and plans for each of our lives, and he invites us to partner with him in pursuing those dreams through prayer, faith, and diligent effort. By seeking God's guidance and direction, clarifying our vision for the future, and setting specific, achievable goals, we can align our lives with his purposes and experience the fulfillment and success that come from walking in obedience to his will.

In this lesson, we will explore the biblical principles of vision and goal-setting, the importance of seeking God's dreams for our lives, and practical strategies for developing and pursuing a vision that honors God and blesses others. By committing our plans to the Lord and trusting in his providence and faithfulness, we can walk confidently into the future, knowing that he is working all things together for our good and his glory.

Discussion Questions

1. What is the difference between vision and goals, and why is it important for Christians to have both in their lives?
2. What are some biblical examples of individuals who had a clear vision for their lives and set goals to achieve them, and how can we apply their principles to our own goal-setting process?
3. What are some practical steps we can take to clarify our vision, set meaningful goals, and pursue God's dreams for our lives, such as prayer, planning, accountability, and perseverance, and how can we trust in God's timing and provision as we work towards our goals?

Lesson 45

Reflecting on Growth and Transformation

Scripture: 2 Corinthians 5:17, Philippians 1:6, Romans 12:2

Memory Verse
- 2 Corinthians 5:17 - "Therefore, if anyone is in Christ, the new creation has come: The old has gone, the new is here!"

Exposition

Reflection is a powerful tool for spiritual growth and transformation, as it allows us to look back on our journey with God, acknowledge our progress, and learn from our experiences. As Christians, we are called to continually grow and mature in our faith, becoming more like Christ in character and conduct. By reflecting on our spiritual journey, recognizing areas of growth and areas needing improvement, and seeking God's guidance and empowerment, we can experience the transformative work of the Holy Spirit in our lives and become more effective disciples and witnesses of Christ to the world.

In this lesson, we will explore the importance of reflection in the Christian life, the biblical principles of growth and transformation, and practical strategies for cultivating a habit of reflection in our spiritual walk. By taking time to evaluate our progress, celebrate our victories, and learn from our mistakes, we can become more intentional and purposeful in our pursuit of God's purposes for our lives.

Discussion Questions

1. Why is reflection important for spiritual growth and transformation, and how does it help us to become more like Christ?
2. What are some biblical examples of individuals who experienced growth and transformation in their spiritual journey, and how can we apply their lessons to our own lives?
3. What are some practical ways we can incorporate reflection into our spiritual practices, such as journaling, prayer, and accountability, and how can we use reflection to deepen our relationship with God and become more effective disciples?

Lesson 46

Overcoming Doubt: Trusting God in Times of Uncertainty

Scripture: James 1:6, Mark 9:24, Proverbs 3:5-6

Memory Verse
- Proverbs 3:5-6 - "Trust in the Lord with all your heart and lean not on your own understanding; in all your ways submit to him, and he will make your paths straight."

Exposition

Doubt is a natural part of the human experience, but as Christians, we are called to trust in God's faithfulness and sovereignty, even in times of uncertainty and adversity. When doubts arise, we can turn to God's Word for assurance, reminding ourselves of his promises and his faithfulness throughout history. By leaning on God's strength and wisdom, surrendering our doubts and fears to him in prayer, and surrounding ourselves with supportive Christian community, we can overcome doubt and walk in confident faith, knowing that God is with us and for us in every circumstance.

In this lesson, we will explore the nature of doubt, the biblical principles of faith and trust in God, and practical strategies for overcoming doubt and strengthening our faith. By cultivating a deeper intimacy with God, grounding ourselves in his Word, and relying on the power of the Holy Spirit, we can find peace and confidence in the midst of uncertainty, and experience the joy and freedom that come from trusting in God's unfailing love and provision.

Discussion Questions

1. What are some common sources of doubt in the Christian life, and how can we respond to doubts in a way that strengthens our faith?

2. What does the Bible teach us about faith and trust in God, and how can we apply these principles to overcome doubt and uncertainty in our lives?

3. What are some practical steps we can take to overcome doubt and strengthen our faith, such as prayer, studying Scripture, seeking wise counsel, and remembering God's faithfulness in the past, and how can we encourage and support one another in our journey of faith?

Lesson 47

Resilience: Bouncing Back from Setbacks with God's Strength

Scripture: Psalm 34:17-18, Isaiah 41:10, Romans 5:3-5

Memory Verse
- Psalm 34:17 - "The righteous cry out, and the Lord hears them; he delivers them from all their troubles."

Exposition

Resilience is the ability to bounce back from setbacks, challenges, and disappointments with faith, strength, and perseverance. As Christians, we are not immune to difficulties, but we have the assurance that God is with us in every trial, empowering us to overcome adversity and grow stronger in our faith. By trusting in God's promises, leaning on his strength, and relying on the support of our Christian community, we can develop resilience that enables us to face life's challenges with courage, hope, and confidence.

In this lesson, we will explore the biblical principles of resilience, the examples of resilience found in Scripture, and practical strategies for cultivating resilience in our own lives.

By drawing near to God in times of trouble, finding strength in his Word, and persevering in prayer and faith, we can navigate life's storms with grace and resilience, and emerge stronger and more steadfast in our walk with God.

Discussion Questions

1. What does resilience mean to you, and why is it important for Christians to develop resilience in their faith journey?
2. What are some biblical examples of individuals who demonstrated resilience in the face of adversity, and what lessons can we learn from their experiences?
3. What are some practical ways we can cultivate resilience in our lives, such as prayer, Scripture meditation, fellowship with believers, and serving others, and how does resilience enable us to grow closer to God and fulfill his purposes for our lives?

Lesson 48

Perseverance in Trials: Finding Hope in the Midst of Adversity

Scripture: James 1:12, Romans 8:28, Hebrews 12:1-2

Memory Verse
- James 1:12 - "Blessed is the one who perseveres under trial because, having stood the test, that person will receive the crown of life that the Lord has promised to those who love him."

Exposition

Perseverance is the steadfast endurance and determination to continue in faith, hope, and obedience to God's will, even in the face of trials and tribulations. As Christians, we are called to persevere in our faith journey, trusting in God's sovereignty, goodness, and faithfulness, and holding fast to the hope we have in Christ. By fixing our eyes on Jesus, the author and perfecter of our faith, we can endure hardship with courage and perseverance, knowing that our trials produce endurance, character, and hope.

In this lesson, we will explore the biblical principles of perseverance, the importance of trusting God's promises in times of trial, and practical strategies for persevering in faith. By embracing our trials as opportunities for growth and drawing near to God in prayer and dependence, we can find hope and strength to persevere through every storm, knowing that God is with us and working all things together for our good.

Discussion Questions

1. Why is perseverance important for Christians, and how does it strengthen our faith and character?
2. What are some biblical examples of individuals who persevered in the midst of trials, and what lessons can we learn from their experiences?
3. What are some practical ways we can cultivate perseverance in our lives, such as prayer, Scripture meditation, fellowship with believers, and serving others, and how does perseverance deepen our trust in God and our reliance on his grace and provision?

Lesson 49

Embracing Change: Surrendering to God's Plan for Your Life

Scripture: Jeremiah 29:11, Isaiah 43:19, Romans 12:2

Memory Verse
- Jeremiah 29:11 - "For I know the plans I have for you," declares the Lord, "plans to prosper you and not to harm you, plans to give you hope and a future."

Exposition

Change is a natural part of life, but it can also be challenging and unsettling, especially when it involves transitions, uncertainties, or unexpected events. As Christians, we are called to embrace change with faith and trust in God's providence and sovereignty, knowing that he is in control and that his plans for us are good and purposeful. By surrendering our plans and desires to God, seeking his guidance and wisdom, and trusting in his faithfulness and provision, we can navigate life's changes with confidence, peace, and hope.

In this lesson, we will explore the biblical principles of embracing change, the promises of God's provision and guidance, and practical strategies for surrendering to God's plan for our lives. By cultivating a posture of humility, flexibility, and dependence on God, we can embrace change as an opportunity for growth, transformation, and deeper intimacy with him.

Discussion Questions

1. How do you typically respond to change, and how does your faith influence your perspective on change?
2. What are some biblical examples of individuals who embraced change and followed God's leading in the midst of uncertainty, and what lessons can we learn from their experiences?
3. What are some practical ways we can surrender to God's plan for our lives and embrace change as an opportunity for growth and transformation, such as prayer, seeking wise counsel, and stepping out in faith, and how does surrendering to God's plan bring peace and fulfillment in our lives?

Lesson 50

Commissioning and Sending Forth into the World to Make Disciples

Scripture: Matthew 28:18-20, Mark 16:15, Acts 1:8

Memory Verse
- Matthew 28:19-20 - "Therefore go and make disciples of all nations, baptizing them in the name of the Father and of the Son and of the Holy Spirit, and teaching them to obey everything I have commanded you. And surely I am with you always, to the very end of the age."

Exposition

As we come to the conclusion of our Sunday School journey, it's essential to reflect on our call as disciples of Christ to go forth and make disciples of all nations. This commission, known as the Great Commission, is at the heart of the Christian faith and mission. Jesus entrusted his followers with the task of spreading the gospel, baptizing believers, and teaching them to obey his commands. As we go forth into the world, we are empowered by the Holy Spirit to share the love of Christ, make disciples, and bring glory to God in all that we do.

In this final lesson, we will explore the significance of the Great Commission, the role of every believer in fulfilling this mission, and practical strategies for sharing the gospel and making disciples in our communities and beyond. By embracing our calling as ambassadors for Christ and following his example of love, service, and sacrifice, we can fulfill our mission with courage, passion, and effectiveness, knowing that Jesus is with us always, empowering and guiding us every step of the way.

Discussion Questions

1. What is the significance of the Great Commission for every believer, and how does it shape our identity and purpose as followers of Christ?
2. What are some practical ways we can fulfill the Great Commission in our daily lives, such as sharing our faith, serving others, and making disciples, and how can we overcome obstacles and fears to be effective witnesses for Christ?
3. How can we support and encourage one another as we go forth into the world to make disciples, and what are some specific steps we can take to fulfill our mission as ambassadors for Christ in our communities, schools, workplaces, and beyond?

As we conclude this Sunday School journey, let us commit ourselves afresh to the mission of making disciples, sharing the gospel, and bringing glory to God in all that we do. May we go forth with confidence, knowing that Jesus is with us always, empowering and guiding us to fulfill his purposes and advance his kingdom in the world. Amen.

Conclusion

As we reach the end of our Sunday School manual journey, let us pause to reflect on the rich lessons we have explored together. From the foundational truths of our faith to the practical wisdom for navigating life's challenges, each lesson has been a stepping stone in our spiritual growth and discipleship journey.

Throughout this journey, we have delved into the depths of Scripture, seeking wisdom and understanding from God's Word. We have grappled with tough questions, wrestled with doubts, and celebrated victories together. We have been challenged to live out our faith boldly, to love extravagantly, and to serve sacrificially.

But our journey does not end here. As we conclude this manual, we are reminded that our call to discipleship is ongoing. We are called to continue growing in our relationship with God, to deepen our understanding of his Word, and to walk in obedience to his commands. We are called to go forth into the world as ambassadors for Christ, sharing the good news of salvation, making disciples, and demonstrating God's love in tangible ways.

As we part ways, let us carry with us the lessons we have learned, the truths we have embraced, and the relationships we have forged. Let us continue to support and encourage one another in our faith journey, knowing that we are not alone, but part of the body of Christ, united in purpose and mission.

May the lessons we have learned in this Sunday School manual empower us to live lives that honor and glorify God, to love others as Christ has loved us, and to make a lasting impact for his kingdom. And may the grace of our Lord Jesus Christ, the love of God, and the fellowship of the Holy Spirit be with us all, now and forevermore. Amen.

Made in United States
Troutdale, OR
09/16/2024

22888880R00066